GRIFFON-SPITFIRE AND SEAFIRE

List by TED HOOTON

ROYAL AIR FORCE SQUADRONS

The following list covers all known squadrons using Griffon-Spitfires from 1943 to 1954. For reasons of clarity, mark numbers are given in arabic numerals. Changes in code letters, or area of operation is shown by two separate lines, as is re-equipment with another type of aircraft or Merlin-Spitfire.

The following abbreviations apply:

Duty:	AAC	Anti-aircraft co-operation.
	F	Fighter and Fighter-bomber.
	FR	Fighter Reconnaissance.
	PR	Photographic-reconnaissance.
	TR	Tactical photo-reconnaissance.
Base:	ETO	North-West Europe, including the United Kingdom.
	FE	India, Burma, Malaya, Hong Kong, and Japan.
	ME	Mediterranean area, including Italy and Palestine.
	UK	United Kingdom only.

SQN.	DUTY	BASE	YEAR	CODE	VERSIONS
1	F	UK	45–46	JX	F.21
2	TR	ETO	44–51	Nil & OI	FR14E PR19
4	TR	ETO	45	Nil	PR19
11	F	FE	45–48	Nil	F14E F18
16	TR	ETO	44–45	Nil	FR14E PR19
17	F	FE	45–48	YB	F14E
20	F	FE	45–46	HN	FR14E
26	TR	ETO	44–46	XC	FR14E
28	F	FE	45–51	Nil	FR14E FR18
32	F	ME	47–49	GZ	FR18
34	PR	FE	46–47	Nil	PR19
41	F	ETO	43–45	EB	F12 F14E
		UK	46–47	EB & Nil	F21
60	F	FE	46–51	Nil	FR14E F18 FR18
73	F	ME	47–48	Nil	F21 F22
80	F	ETO	48–49	W2	F24
		FE	49–51	W2	F24
81	PR	FE	47–54	Nil	FR18 PR19
91	F	UK	43–44	DL	F12 F14 F14E
			45–46	DL	F21
122	F	UK	45–46	MT	F21
129	F	UK	45	DV	F14E
130	F	ETO	44–45	AP	F14 F14E
132	F	FE	45–46	FF	F14E
136	F	FE	45–46	HM	F14E
152	F	FE	45–46	UM	F14E
155	F	FE	45–46	DG	F14E
208	FR	ME	47–51	RG	FR18
268	TR	ETO	44–45	Nil	FR14E PR19
273	F	FE	45	MS	FR14E
322	F	UK	44	3W	F14 F14E
350	F	UK	44	MN	F14
		ETO	44–45	MN	F14E
401	F	ETO	44–45	YO	F14E
402	F	ETO	44–45	AE	F14E
411	F	ETO	45–46	DB	F14E
412	F	ETO	45–46	VZ	F14E
414	FR	ETO	45	Nil	F12* FR14E
416	F	ETO	45–46	DN	F14E
430	FR	ETO	44–45	G9?	F12* FR14E
443	F	ETO	45–46	2I	F14E
451	FR	ETO	45–46	NI	FR14E
453	F	ETO	45–46	FU	F14E
502	F	UK	49–50	RAC	F22
			50–51	V9	F22
504	F	UK	48–50	RAD	F22
			50	TM	F22
541	PR	UK	44–45	Nil	PR19
			46	ES	PR19
			47–51	WY	PR19
542	PR	UK	44–45	Nil	PR19
595	AAC	UK	44–45	7B	F12*
600	F	UK	46–50	RAG	FR14E F21 F22
602	F	UK	46–47	LO	FR14E
			46–50	RAI	FR14E F21 F22
			50–51	LO	F21 F22
603	F	UK	47–50	RAJ	F21 F22
			50–51	XT & Nil	F22
607	F	FE	45	AF	F14E
		UK	47–50	RAN	FR14E F22
			50–51	LA	F22
608	F	UK	48–50	RAQ	F22
			50	6T	F22
610	F	ETO	44–45	DW	F14 F14E
		UK	46–50	RAQ	FR14E F21 F22
			50–51	DW	F22
611	F	UK	46–50	RAR	FR14E F22
			50–51	FY	F22
612	F	UK	46–48	RAS	FR14E
613	F	UK	46–50	RAT	FR14E F21 F22
			50–51	Q3	F22
614	F	UK	48–50	RAU	F22
			50	7A	F22
615	F	UK	46–50	RAV	FR14E F21 F22
			50	V6	F22
616	F	UK	49–50	RAW	F22
681	PR	FE	45–46	Nil	PR19
682	PR	ME	44–46	Nil	PR19
683	TR	ME	45	Nil	FR14E
691	AAC	UK	45	5S	F14

**Few for training*

Other users:

8	OTU Photo-reconnaissance (later 237 OCU)	BE LP
61	OTU Fighter (later 226 OCU)	DE UU
102	Flying Refresher School	Nil
111	OTU Coastal	3G
226	OCU Fighter	UU XL
237	OCU Photo-reconnaissance	LP
1335	Conversion Unit (To 226 OCU in 1947)	XL
	Aircraft & Armament Experimental Establishment	Nil
	Air Fighting Development Unit (later C.F.E.)	GO
	Central Bomber Establishment	DF
	Central Fighter Establishment	GO JW UX
	Photographic Reconnaissance Development Unit	6C

Royal Indian Air Force and Indian Air Force.

As far as is known no code letters were used by the squadrons. With the exception of 101 sqn., all were fighter units.

1 sqn.	45–47	F14E	8 sqn.	46–47	F14E
2 sqn.	45–48	F14E	9 sqn.	46–47	F14E
3 sqn.	46	F14E	14 sqn.	51–55	FR18
6 sqn.	46–47	FR14E	101 sqn.	51–55	PR19

SEAFIRE SQUADRONS

The listing follows the same format as for the RAF Spitfires except that separate lines are shown for each change of carrier. Land bases are not shown unless particularly significant. Also, with the exception of squadrons 816 to 842 which were combined Seafire/Swordfish units for convoy protection, all 800–series units were fighter squadrons. Code letters are not shown because many duplications occurred and variations in style were common.

The basic code system consisted of a letter/number/letter format indicating: Carrier code/Aircraft class/Individual aircraft letter. Single-seat fighters made up one aircraft class and thus Seafires used the numbers: 5, 6, 7, and 8. However, the variations of format were numerous. As an example, 807 squadron used the following codes on their Seafires:

T	Aircraft 'T', HMS Furious, 1942.
7 K	Aircraft 'K', HMS Indomitable, 1943.
8 M	Aircraft 'M', HMS Battler, 1943.
HL	Aircraft 'L', HMS Hunter, 1943–44 (Code 'H')
D5 V	Aircraft 'V', HMS Hunter, 1945 (Code 'D', also used by HMS Stalker—D6, 809 sqn.).

On 31.3.45, the R.N. carriers with the U.S. Pacific Fleet adopted the American style of markings. This involved changes to the roundels and code letters. Thus, Seafires on the Implacable and Indefatigable carried the tail letters 'N' and 'S' respectively, and had three-digit fuselage numbers beginning with '1'. This system was extended to all R.N. aircraft after the war.

SQN.	AREA	YEAR	CARRIER	VERSIONS
800	UK ME FE	46–50	Triumph	F15 F17 FR47
801	UK ME	42–44	Furious	IB 2C
	UK FE	44–46	Implacable	3 F15
	UK	47	Land	F17
802	UK	45	Premier	F15
		46	Berwick	F15
		47	Vengeance	F17
803	UK CAN	45–47	Warrior	F15
804	UK	46–47	Theseus	F15
		47	Ocean	F15
		48–49	Glory	FR47
805	FE	45–46	Land	3
	UK ME	46	Ocean	F15
	UK	47–48	Land	F17
806	UK	45	Berwick	F15
		46	Glory	F15
807	UK ME	42–43	Furious	1B 2C
	UK ME	43	Indomitable	2C
	ME	43	Battler	2C
	ME UK FE	43–45	Hunter	2C 3
	UK	46	Implacable	F17
		47	Vengeance	F17
808	UK ME	42–43	Battler	1B 2C
	ME UK	43	Hunter	2C
	UK	44	Land	3
809	UK ME	43	Unicorn	2C
	UK ME FE	43–45	Stalker	3
	UK	45–46	Land	F17
816	UK	43	Tracker	2C
833	UK ME	43	Stalker	2C 3
834	UK ME	43	Hunter	2C
	ME UK	43–44	Battler	2C 3
842	UK	43	Fencer	2C
879	UK ME FE	43–45	Attacker	2C 3
880	UK ME	42–43	Argus	1B
	UK	43	Indomitable	2C
			Stalker	2C
		44	Furious	2C
	UK FE	44–45	Implacable	3
883	CAN	47–48	Land	F15
884	UK	42–43	Argus	2C
885	UK ME	42–43	Formidable	1B 2C
	UK	44	Land	3
886	UK	43	Attacker	2C
	UK	44	Land	2C 3
887	UK ME	42–43	Unicorn	1 B2C
	UK FE	44–46	Indefatigable	3
889	FE	44–45	Land	3
	FE	45	Indomitable	3
894	UK ME	43	Illustrious	2C 3
	UK	44	Land/Implacable	3
	UK FE	44–46	Indefatigable	3
897	UK	43	Unicorn	2C
	UK ME	43	Stalker	2C
	ME UK	43–44	Land	2C 3
899	UK ME	43	Indomitable	2C
	ME	43	Hunter	3
	UK ME	44	Khedive	3
	UK ME	45	Chaser	3

Reserve squadrons.

Land based in the U.K., with occasional short periods on various carriers during summer training:

1831	Stretton	47–51	F17
1832	Culham	47–51	F17 FR17 FR46
1833	Bramcote	47–53	F17 FR47

Second-line units.

All training units with the exception of 728, 771, and 775, which were Fleet Requirements Units. All based in U.K. except for 728 Malta; 775 Egypt; 778 India up to 1946–also 787 squadron.

701	3 F15	759	F17 FR47	771	3 F45
715	3 F15	761	3	773	F15
718	3 F15	764	F17	775	2C 3
728	2C 3	766	F17	778	F15 F17 F45
736	F17	767	F15 F17	781	F46
738	F17 F46	770	3 F15	787	F17

FR.XIV, No. 28 Squadron, SEAC, Kuala Lampur, Malaya, 1945. Standard Green/Grey scheme

SUPERMARINE SPITFIRE MK.XII-24

SUPERMARINE SEAFIRE MK.I-47

Illustrated by Richard Ward

Compiled by Ted Hooton and Richard Ward

Text by Ted Hooton

ACKNOWLEDGMENTS

Grateful thanks are extended to all who assisted with photographs and information making possible the publication of this pictorial survey of the Griffon engined Spitfire and brief coverage of the Merlin and Griffon engined Seafire. Thanks to all those who assisted whose names are listed below in alphabetical order.

L. Bachelor, F. Baratelli, Canadian Dept. National Defence, Etablissement Cinematographique des Armees, Flight International, F. G. Freeman Jr., M. Garbett, J. Harvey, H. Holmes, T. Hooton, Irish Air Corps, Imperial War Museum, R. C. Jones IPMS, Swedish Air Force, G. J. Thomas.

F.XIV, No. 132 'City of Bombay' Squadron, SEAC, Malaya, 1945. Standard Green/Grey scheme but without white wing bands.

PUBLISHED BY

Arco Publishing Company, Inc., 219 Park Avenue South, New York, N.Y. 10003

First Published by Osprey Publications Ltd. and Printed in Great Britain

Library of Congress No. 73-93930 · Library Edition SBN 668-02109-8 · Paperback Edition SBN 668-02107-1

Nice flying shot of a pair of Mk. XII's of No. 41 Squadron, sky spinner, code and fuselage band, note yellow leading edge stripe. (IWM).

Good clear shot showing the changed nose lines of the first Griffon engined variant, the Mk.XII. (IWM).

GRIFFON-SPITFIRES Mk.XII, XIV, and XVIII to 24

In 1939 the Supermarine design team under J. Smith began work on the Spitfire Mk. IV around the projected Rolls-Royce Type 37 engine, later known as the Griffon. The early war years delayed both airframe and engine, but in 1941 two prototypes were ordered, and by 1942, when they took to the air, they had been re-designated as the Spitfire Mk. XX(DP845) and Mk. XXI(DP851).

From these beginnings, and through subsequent development of the Mk. VIII airframe, came a variety of Griffon-Spitfires. The Mk. 21-24 series was almost a new type of aircraft, having a completely new wing design; the Mk. XII, XIV, and XIX being interim developments; while the Mk. XVIII was a later version of the XIV with different wing construction.

Large-scale production began in 1944 and just over two thousand were built up to 1948 (nearly half were Mk. XIV's). They were never employed in combat to the extent of the Merlin-Spitfires but, nevertheless, saw service with sixty squadrons of the R.A.F. and R.Aux.A.F. between 1943 and 1954. Peak operational strength was in 1945 when some twenty squadrons were equipped. They were also used by the air forces of ten foreign countries, and not until 1957 did the last Griffon-Spitfire retire from useful flying duties.

Compared with their Merlin counterparts they were quite a different aircraft in many ways, partially due to the opposite engine rotation of the Griffon and aerodynamic design changes. But, although they lost the "sweetness" of the original Spitfires, they still remained a favourite with their pilots.

Wartime Service 1943 to 1945

This period saw the operational use of the Spitfire Mk. XII, XIV, XIX, and 21.

The Mk. XII was a 1942 "panic" conversion of the basic Mk. VIII/IX airframe with a low-altitude rated Griffon and clipped wings, and was based on experience derived from the Spitfire Mk. XX prototype. It was ordered to counter the menace of the Luftwaffe's Fw190 "tip-and-run" raids on the south coast of England and, built in small numbers, first entered service with 41 squadron in January 1943, followed by 91 squadron in April. Low-altitude patrols and, later, offensive sweeps were the speciality of the two squadrons, but during 1943 development of the Mk. XIV proceeded apace. This variant was intended for all-altitude fighting, being fitted with a two-stage supercharged Griffon. Initially produced with the "C" wing, it first went into service with 350 (Belgian) and 610 squadrons in January 1944, followed by 91 and 322 a few months later.

Intended for the defence of the D-day beachheads, the Spitfire XIV was diverted from that role to join the Tempest and Mustang in defending London against the German V1 flying bomb offensive which began in mid-June. Thus it was that 91, 322, and 610, together with 41 squadron (Mk. XII), shot down more than three hundred of the 429 V1's claimed by Spitfires. No. 91 squadron was the most successful, while Lt. Burgwal of 322 (Dutch) squadron was the highest-scoring Spitfire pilot with 21 claims.

In September, with the V1 menace subsiding, 130 squadron, newly-equipped with the F.XIVE, went to the 2nd Tactical Air Force on the Continent, and in December was joined by 350 and 610 to form No. 125 Wing. In the following March, 41 squadron replaced 610, and the Wing was kept busy on both fighter and ground-attack operations until the end of the War in Europe in May, 1945. During this time a number of Ar234 and Me262 jets were shot down.

Meanwhile, the Spitfire FR.XIVE and PR.XIX had entered service for reconnaissance duties. The PR.XIX was rushed into production with an order for twenty-two aircraft (RM626-647), these being unarmed Mk. XIV's with extra fuel in the wings and fuselage-mounted cameras. They entered service with 541/542 squadrons in England around the time of D-day, and some reached 682 squadron in Italy in the late autumn.

The Spitfire FR.XIVE was a popular aircraft with 20mm. cannon and .5 in. machine-guns, "tear-drop" canopy, clipped wings, and oblique camera. It came into service with 2nd T.A.F. in the early autumn of 1944 replacing the Mustang I's of 2, 268, and 430 squadrons.

Finally in early 1945, 1 and 91 squadrons in England

Formation of Mk. XII's by No. 41 Squadron, in the upper photograph the larger spinner is very obvious. H is MB794, D MB858. (photos IWM).

The first Spitfire Mk. XII, EN221. The wings were not clipped on this aircraft so that comparative tests could be run with EN222 which did have clipped wings. Both aircraft were flown by Flt.Lt. 'Spud' Potocki at the Intensive Flying Development Unit, Boscombe Down, December 1942.

re-equipped with the new Spitfire F.21, but only a few bomber escort sorties were flown before the end of hostilities.

As the War in Europe ended, many F/FR.XIVE aircraft were sent to the Far East, and in Burma 20, 132, and 273 squadrons were amongst the first units to re-equip, early in 1945. With the Japanese Army Air Force already reduced to an ineffective level, ground attack sorties were the order of the day, except for 681 squadron which received a few PR.XIX (later production models with a pressurised cockpit) as the War ended in August.

Post war 1946 to 1954

In Europe, the regular R.A.F. squadrons with Griffon-Spitfires were soon disbanded or re-equipped with other types. Notable exceptions were 2 squadron in Germany which operated both the FR.14E* and PR.19 until 1951, as did 541 squadron with the PR.19 in England, both units performing many useful photo surveys during that time.

However, the R.Aux.A.F. employed the Griffon-Spitfire in some numbers between 1946 and 1951. A few squadrons having the FR.14E as initial equipment received F.21's in 1947, but in 1948-49 the F.22 (basically a F.21 with "tear-drop" canopy and revised fin/rudder) became the most widely used fighter. No. 603, 607, 611, and 613 squadrons still had F.22's during the 1951 reserve call-up.

Meanwhile, in 1947 the Spitfire Mk.18 entered service in overseas units. In Palestine, the FR.18 equipped 32 and 208 squadrons and both units were involved in combat with Egyptian and Israeli Spitfire 9's. In the Far East, the F.18 and FR.18 replaced the Mk.14E, many of the latter being transferred to the Royal Indian Air Force and subsequently used against Pakistan in the fighting that followed the partition of India.

The R.A.F. Mk.18's were employed against the Communist guerillas in Malaya by 28 and 60 squadrons, the former being transferred to Hong Kong in 1949 and joined there by 80 squadron with the Spitfire F.24 (essentially a ground-attack variant of the F.22). All this time 81 squadron (ex-681/34 squadron) provided photo-reconnaissance for the entire area, and one of their PR.19's flew the last operational sortie of an R.A.F. Spitfire on April 1st, 1954.

Apart from the eight squadrons of the Indian Air Force, the greatest use of the Griffon-Spitfires by foreign countries was by Belgium with F/FR.14's in eight squadrons between 1947 and 1952, and by Sweden which took delivery of fifty PR.19's in 1948-49 for F.11 Wing at Nyköping.

* Up to late 1942 all mark numbers were in Roman numerals. From 1943 to 1948 arabic numbers were used for twenty-one or greater. From 1948 all mark numbers used arabic style. For ease of reference the latter is used here for the entire post war period.

Good side view showing the new nose lines of the Mk. XII, MB882 of No. 41 Squadron. (IWM).

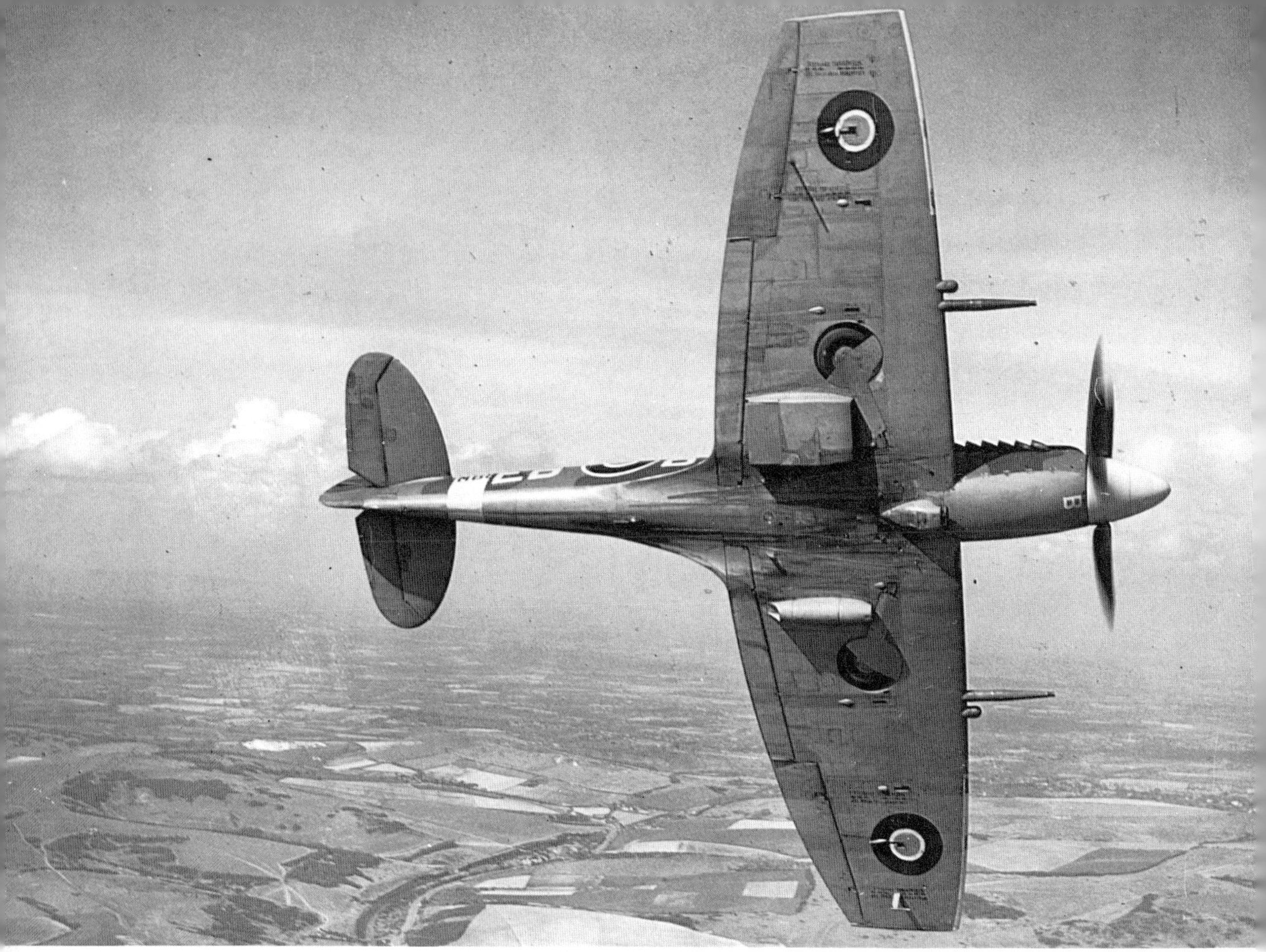

Upper and under surface detail shots of MB882 of No. 41 Squadron. (IWM).

Above: Mk. XIV's of No. 610 'County of Chester' Squadron, spring 1944. DW–D, RB159 is the CO's aircraft, note pennant under windscreen.

Right & below: Starboard side views of DW–D, sky spinner, code and fuselage stripe. (photos IWM).

Formation of Mk. XIV's of No. 610 'County of Chester' Squadron, spring 1944. (IWM).

Above: NH169 of the Central Fighter Establishment, West Raynham, firing rockets. (Flight International).

Above: F.XIVE, RM704 of the Central Fighter Establishment, West Raynham, 1946. Both aircraft with black and white spinners, sky codes and fuselage bands. (via L. Bachelor).

Below: FR.XIVE, TZ138, in Canada for cold-weather testing at Edmonton, 1945–46. (F. Bartelli).

Above: FR.XIVE, of No. 2 Squadron, 2nd TAF, Germany 1945–46. (F. Henley via R. C. Jones).

Above: FR.XIVE, TZ112 of No. 2 Squadron, 2nd TAF, 1948. Code OI–G. Natural metal finish, black band on spinner.

Below: FR.XIVE's and PR.19 s of No. 2 Squadron, 2nd TAF at Wahn, Germany, 1948–49. (Flight International).

F.XIV of No. 41 Squadron, No. 125 Wing, 2nd TAF, Germany. Serial RM653. (via R. C. Jones).

F.XIV, No. 402 RCAF Squadron, note sky fuselage band has been painted over. Serial RN119. (IWM).

Above & below: F.XIV's, No. 130 'Punjab' Squadron on a Belgian airfield, Dec. 1944. Invasion stripes under the fuselage only. (photos IWM).

Right: F.XIV, No. 17 Squadron, Seletar, Singapore 1945. YB–O, RN972, note serial in white under fin flash. (D. K. Healey via G. J. Thomas).

Left: Close-up of nose detail of YB–O, D. K. Healey with ground crew. (D. K. Healey via G. J. Thomas)

Below: YB–C, RN205 flying off HMS Trumpeter bound for Kelanang, Malaya, Sept. 1945. (via G. J. Thomas).

Below: FR.XIVE, No. 28 Squadron, Kaula Lampur, Malaya, 1946. (G. J. Thomas).

FR.XIVE, No. 28 Squadron, MV349 flown by Sgt. D. McPhail. (D. McPhail via G. J. Thomes).

Line-up of No. 28 Sqdn. F.XIVE's at Kuala Lampur, 1946. H, NH869; T, SM893. Green/earth camouflage. (G. J. Thomas).

Above: MV320, X, No. 28 Squadron, Kuala Lampur, 1946. Green/earth camouflage. (G. J. Thomas).

Below: F.XVIII, No. 28 Squadron, over Malaya. Serial TP377. (D. McPhail via G. J. Thomas).

Above: F.XIV, No. 152 Squadron in scrap yard. See colour illustration.

Left: Close-up of No. 152 Squadron insignia. (W. Power).

Below: FR.XIVE, No. 273 Squadron, Malaya. (IWM).

Below: F.XIV's, No. 132 'City of Bombay' Squadron, see colour illustration. (IWM).

ght: F.XIV's being taken ashore at ng Kong, 1945. Good shot showing mouflage pattern, position and size national insignia. (IWM).

low: Nose detail of No. 132 Squadron craft. (via R. C. Jones).

Below: FR.XVIII, No. 32 Squadron, Serial TZ220. Middle East.
(J. Old via R. C. Jones).

Above: FR.XVIII, No. 32 Squadron in the Middle East, note the hunting horn insignia under cockpit. As seen on this and preceding photograph it was common practice to remove the oblique camera on FR type aircraft, the port being covered with fabric. TP373.

Right: One of the last F.XVIII's built, TP235 is seen here in Malaya and was probably with No. 60 Squadron. (via L. Bachelor).

Above: One of the PR.XIX's from the first production batch without pressurisation, RM645 is seen here with No. 682 Squadron, Italy, in early 1945. (via L. Bachelor).

Right: RM643 Z of No. 541 Squadron, Benson late 1944. First production batch without pressurisation, D-Day Invasion stripes on fuselage only. (via R. C. Jones).

Below: PR19, OI–X PM627 of No. 2 Squadron, 2nd TAF in Germany.

Above: PR.19, PS852 of No. 81 Squadron on detachment at Hong Kong,1952–53(Flight International).

Right: PR.19, PM631 'Thum' Flight, Speke Airport, 1956. Note crudely painted serial. (R. L. Ward via R. C. Jones).

Above: Low-level beat-up by PR.19 PS 890 at Seletar, Singapore. This aircraft later went to the Royal Thai Air Force, see colour illustration. (Flight International).

Right: PR.19, PM655, 6C–W of the Photographic Reconnaissance Development Unit, 1947–48. This aircraft was also coded 6C–X after the roundel change to pre-war type.

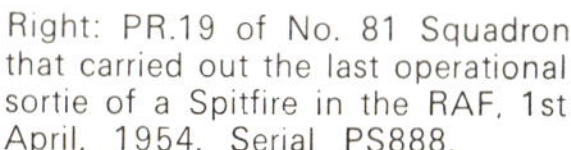
Right: PR.19 of No. 81 Squadron that carried out the last operational sortie of a Spitfire in the RAF, 1st April, 1954. Serial PS888.

Formation of F.21's of No. 600 'City of London' Squadron, R.Aux.A.F., RAG–J LA328. (photos Flight International).

F.21's of No. 600 'City of London' Squadron, R.Aux.A.F., standard camouflage and yellow wing leading edge stripe. (photos Flight International).

Above: Early production F.21, LA195 of No. 615 'County of Surrey' Squadron, R.Aux.A.F. (Flight International).
Below: Mixed formation of F.21's and F.22's of No. 600 'City of London' Squadron, R.Aux.A.F. (Flight International).

Above: Under surface detail of F.21 LA195 of No. 600 Squadron. (Flight International).

Right: F.22 of No. 607 'County of Durham' Squadron R.Aux.A.F., in race markings. (RAF/MOD).

Above: F.22's of No. 613 'East Lancashire' Squadron, R.Aux.A.F., note squadron crest above fin flash. RAT–E PK331. (Flight International).

Right: One of the few F.21's to have contra-props, No. 41 Squadron, July 1947, see colour illustration. (via F. G. Freeman Jr.).

Top two pictures: F.XIVE, SG66 of No. 350 Squadron, Belgian Air Force. Note presentation of serial on under surfaces. Beauvrechain, 1947–48.

Above: FR.XIVE, SG56 of No. 380 Squadron, Belgian Air Force.

Above: & below: FR.XIVE's of No. 1 Squadron, No. 2 Wing, Belgian Air Force, Florennes, 1947–. Standard RAF camouflage, black spinners.

Mixed Spitfires of No. 1 Squadron, No. 2 Wing, Florennes, BAF. Note variations in the presentation of the squadron insignia.

Above & right: Line-up of FR.XIVE's of No. 2 Squadron, No. 2 Wing, Florennes, BAF. Note variations in presentation of code and Comet insignia on nose.

Below: F.XIVE of No. 2 Squadron. On bare metal aircraft it was the usual practice to paint the cannon blisters black.

Below: F.XIVE, of No. 3 Squadron, No. 2 Wing, Florennes. No. 2 Wing flew Spitfires from 1947 to 1952. Details of the Wing and Squadron Insignia will be found on the Unit Insignia plate in AIRCAM No. 5.

Below: Camouflaged F.XIVE of No. 3 Squadron at Florennes in 1948. Florennes was built by the Luftwaffe in 1941-42 as a night-fighter base and the remains of a Me.410 can be seen to the right. Note Holly Leaf insignia on cowl.

A

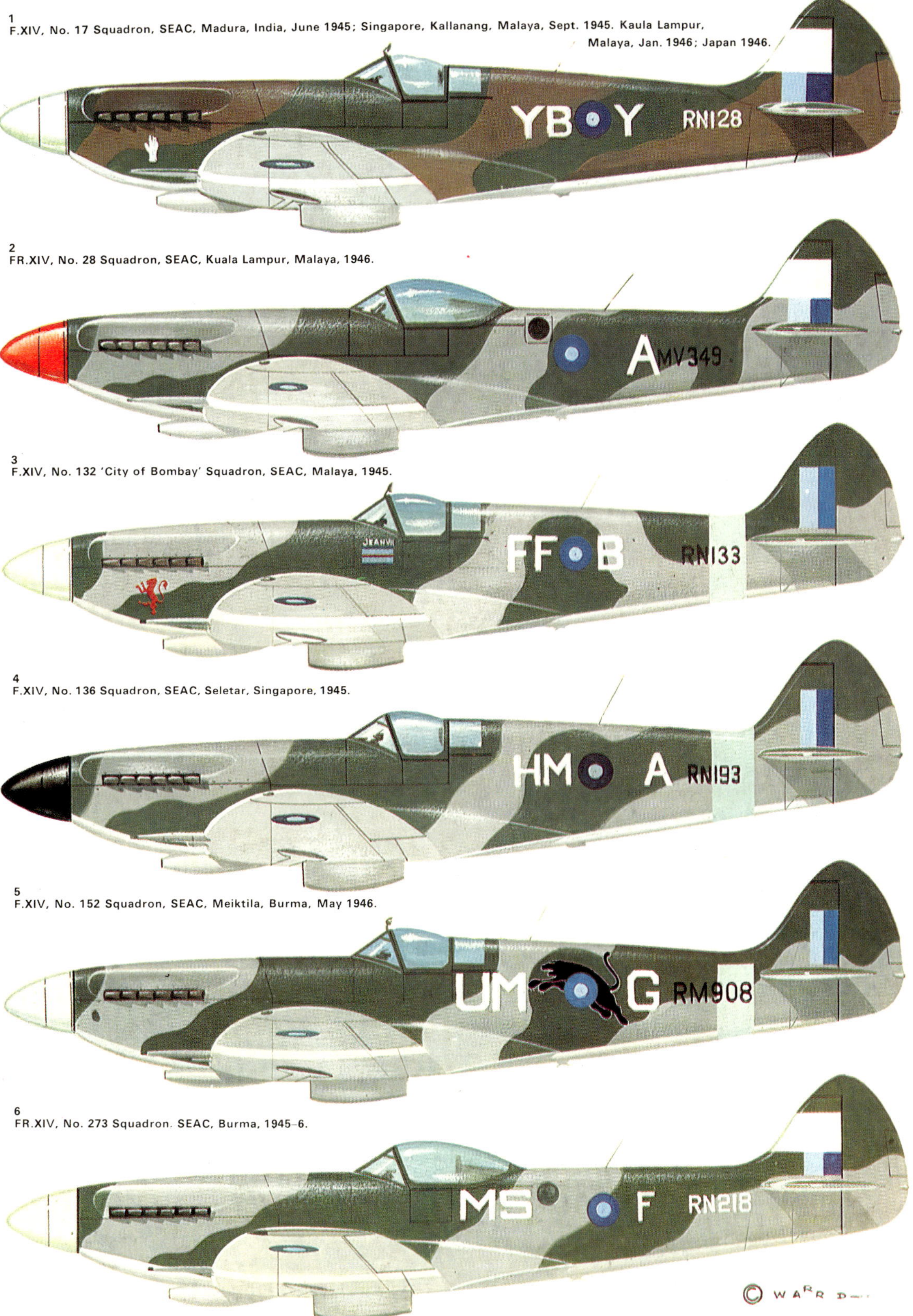

1
F.XIV, No. 17 Squadron, SEAC, Madura, India, June 1945; Singapore, Kallanang, Malaya, Sept. 1945. Kaula Lampur, Malaya, Jan. 1946; Japan 1946.

2
FR.XIV, No. 28 Squadron, SEAC, Kuala Lampur, Malaya, 1946.

3
F.XIV, No. 132 'City of Bombay' Squadron, SEAC, Malaya, 1945.

4
F.XIV, No. 136 Squadron, SEAC, Seletar, Singapore, 1945.

5
F.XIV, No. 152 Squadron, SEAC, Meiktila, Burma, May 1946.

6
FR.XIV, No. 273 Squadron. SEAC, Burma, 1945–6.

B

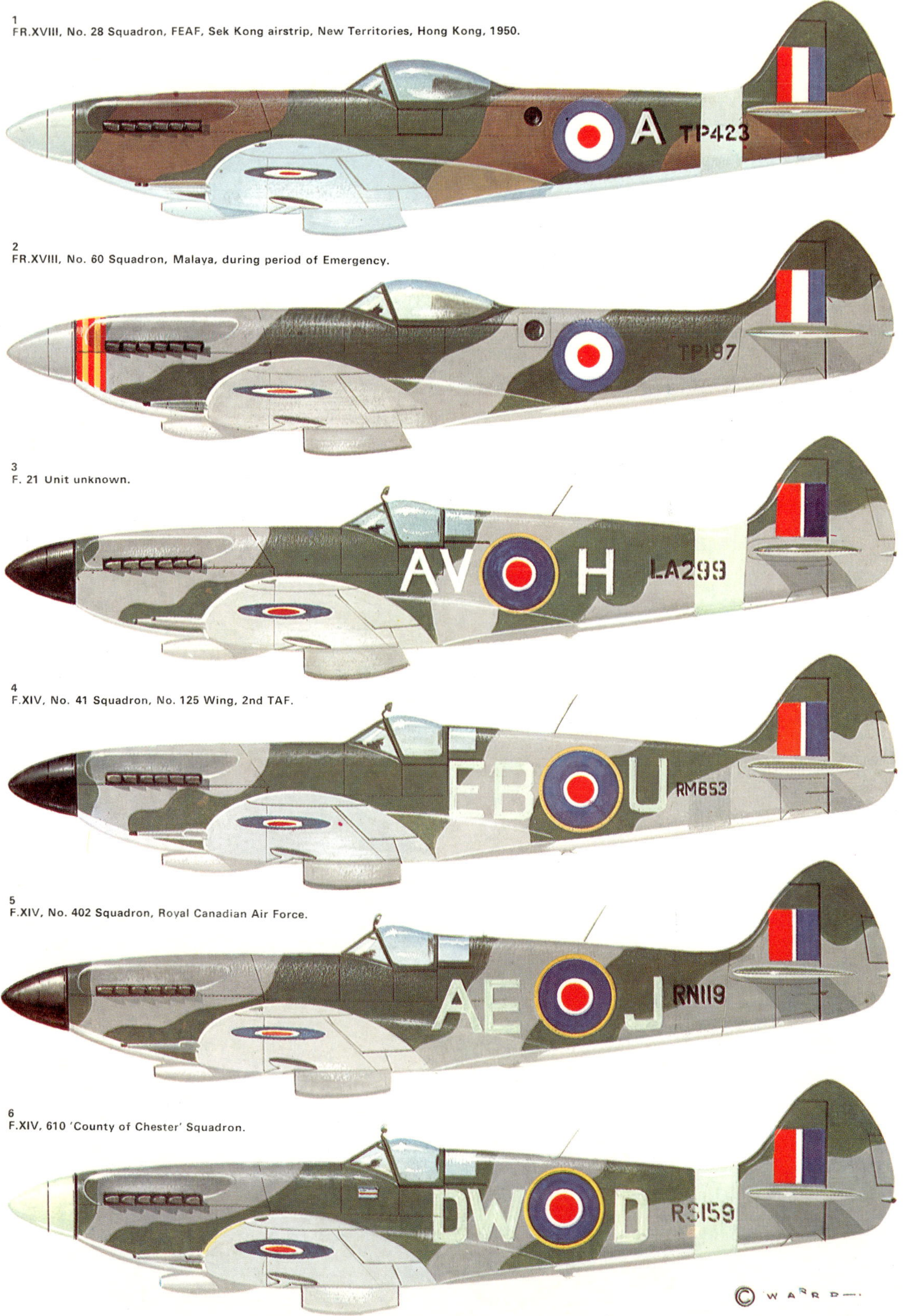

1
FR.XVIII, No. 28 Squadron, FEAF, Sek Kong airstrip, New Territories, Hong Kong, 1950.

2
FR.XVIII, No. 60 Squadron, Malaya, during period of Emergency.

3
F. 21 Unit unknown.

4
F.XIV, No. 41 Squadron, No. 125 Wing, 2nd TAF.

5
F.XIV, No. 402 Squadron, Royal Canadian Air Force.

6
F.XIV, 610 'County of Chester' Squadron.

C

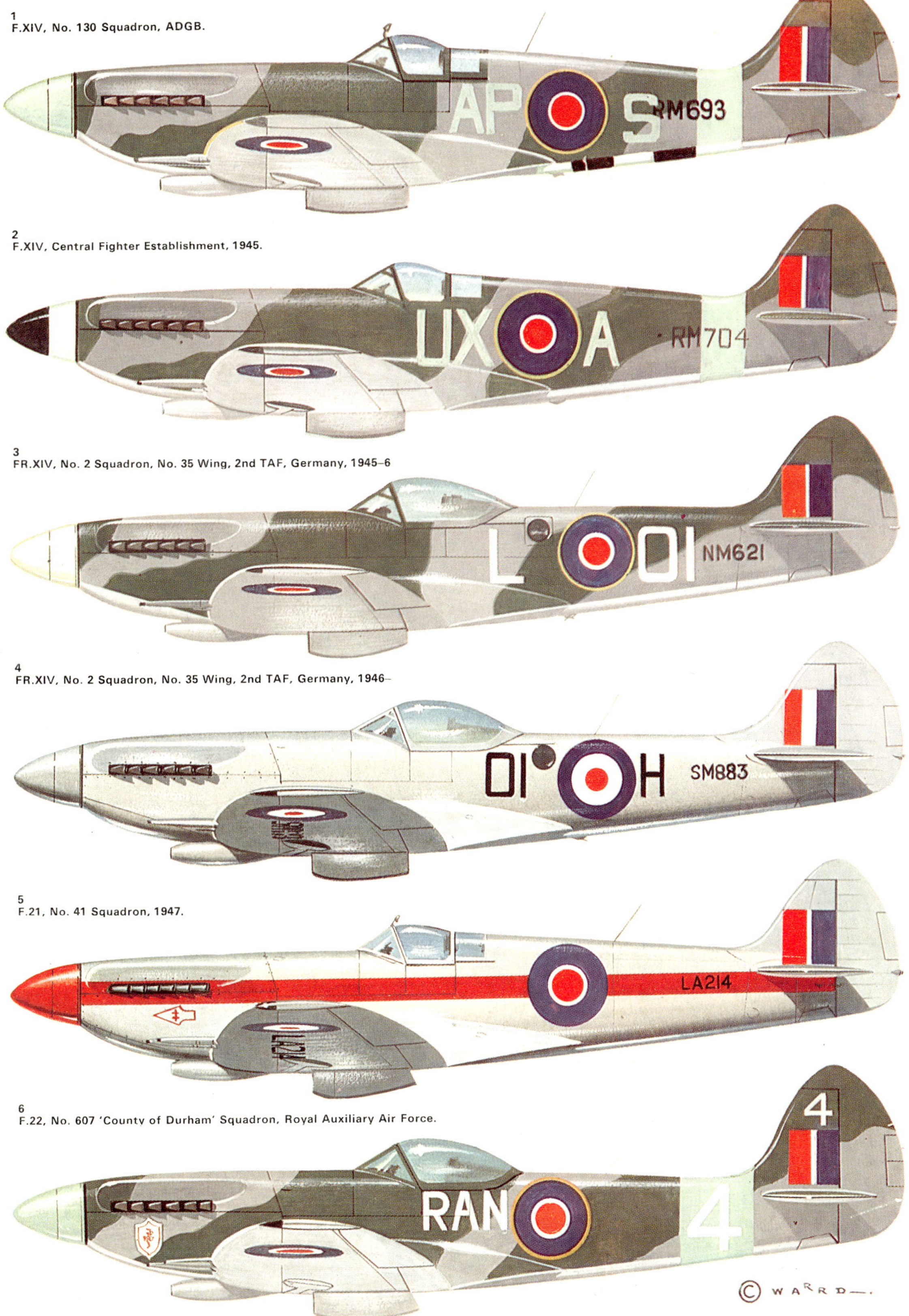

1
F.XIV, No. 130 Squadron, ADGB.

2
F.XIV, Central Fighter Establishment, 1945.

3
FR.XIV, No. 2 Squadron, No. 35 Wing, 2nd TAF, Germany, 1945–6

4
FR.XIV, No. 2 Squadron, No. 35 Wing, 2nd TAF, Germany, 1946–

5
F.21, No. 41 Squadron, 1947.

6
F.22, No. 607 'County of Durham' Squadron, Royal Auxiliary Air Force.

D

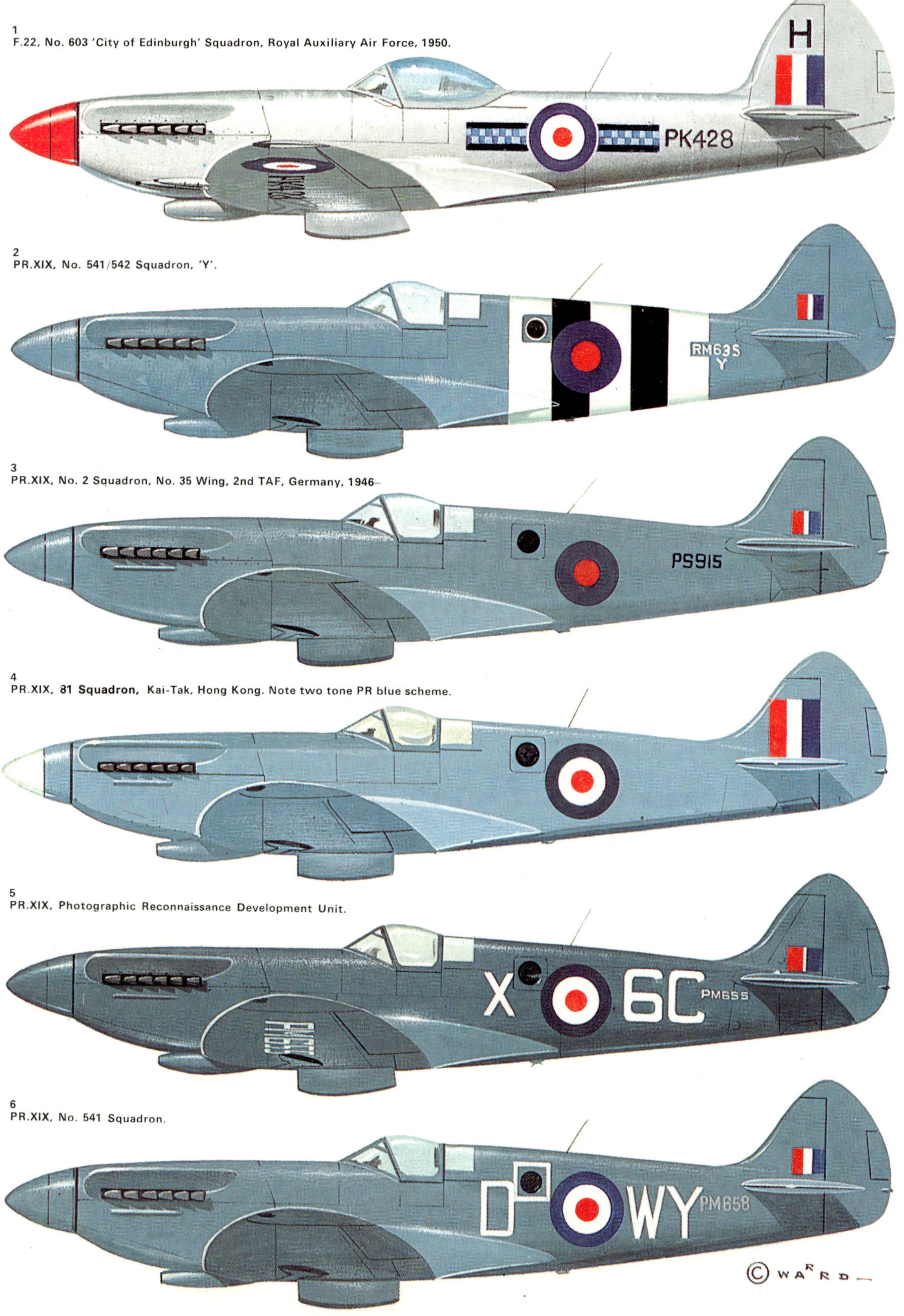

1
F.22, No. 603 'City of Edinburgh' Squadron, Royal Auxiliary Air Force, 1950.

2
PR.XIX, No. 541/542 Squadron, 'Y'.

3
PR.XIX, No. 2 Squadron, No. 35 Wing, 2nd TAF, Germany, 1946–

4
PR.XIX, **81 Squadron,** Kai-Tak, Hong Kong. Note two tone PR blue scheme.

5
PR.XIX, Photographic Reconnaissance Development Unit.

6
PR.XIX, No. 541 Squadron.

E

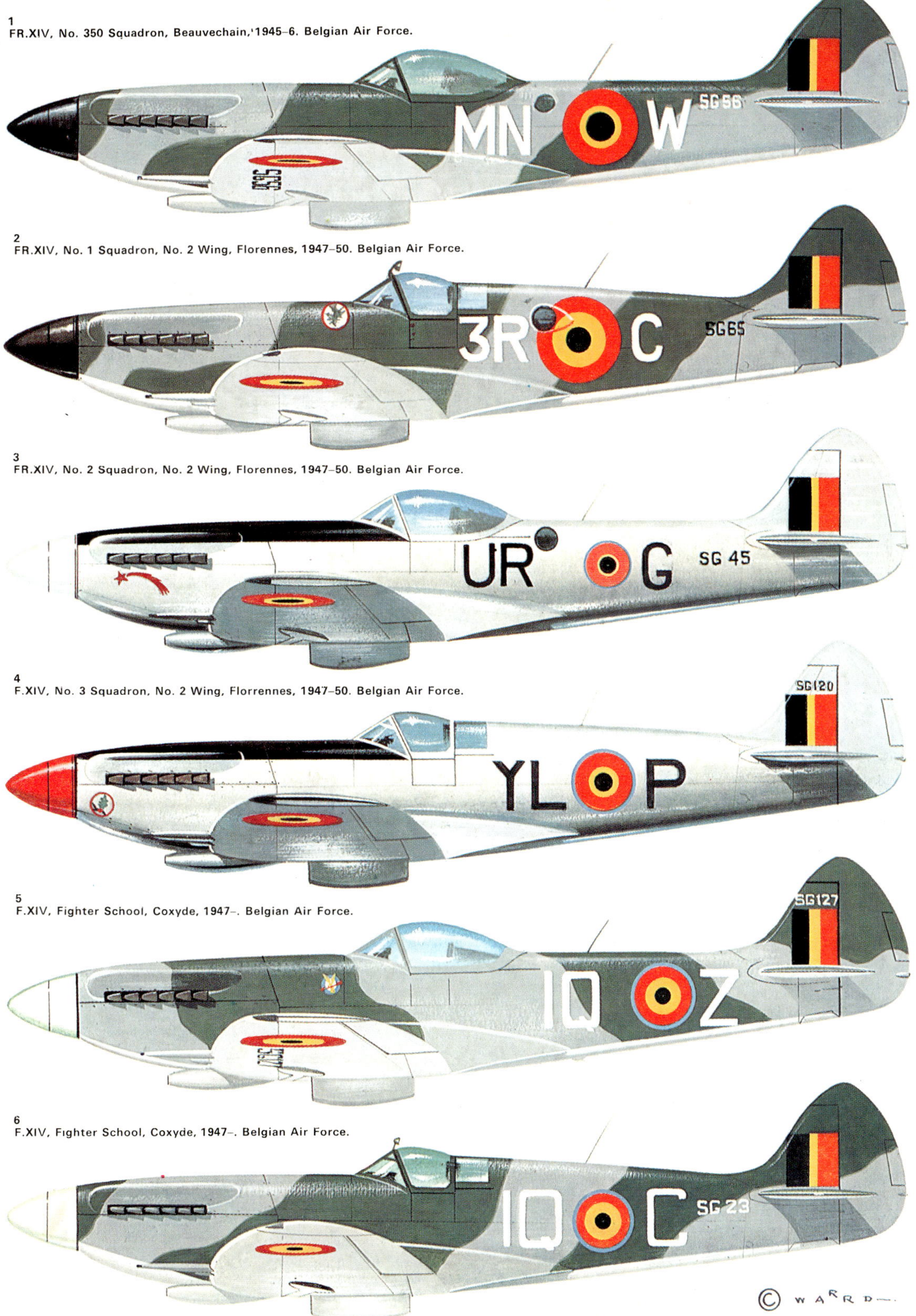

1
FR.XIV, No. 350 Squadron, Beauvechain, 1945–6. Belgian Air Force.

2
FR.XIV, No. 1 Squadron, No. 2 Wing, Florennes, 1947–50. Belgian Air Force.

3
FR.XIV, No. 2 Squadron, No. 2 Wing, Florennes, 1947–50. Belgian Air Force.

4
F.XIV, No. 3 Squadron, No. 2 Wing, Florrennes, 1947–50. Belgian Air Force.

5
F.XIV, Fighter School, Coxyde, 1947–. Belgian Air Force.

6
F.XIV, Fighter School, Coxyde, 1947–. Belgian Air Force.

F

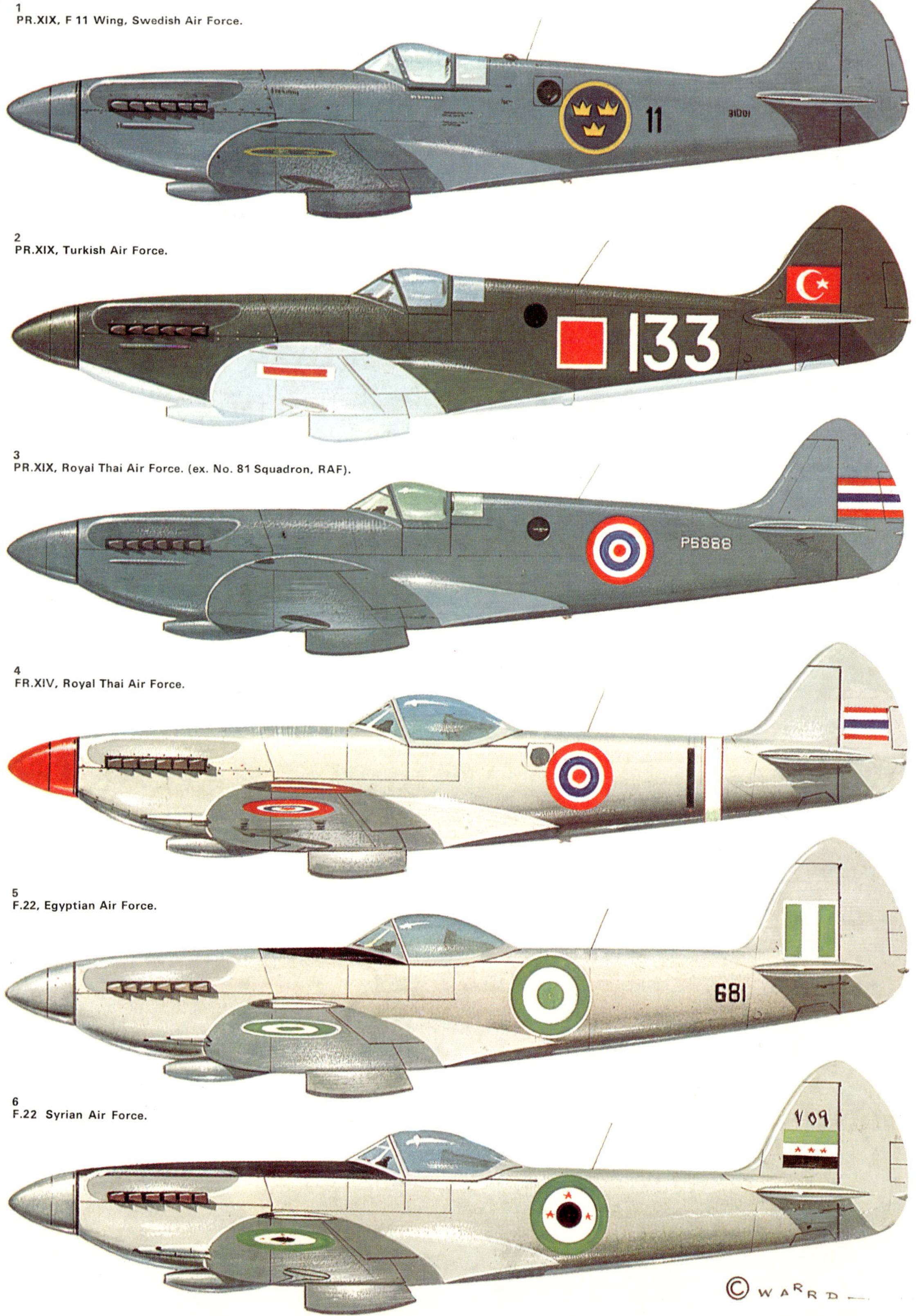

1
PR.XIX, F 11 Wing, Swedish Air Force.

2
PR.XIX, Turkish Air Force.

3
PR.XIX, Royal Thai Air Force. (ex. No. 81 Squadron, RAF).

4
FR.XIV, Royal Thai Air Force.

5
F.22, Egyptian Air Force.

6
F.22 Syrian Air Force.

G

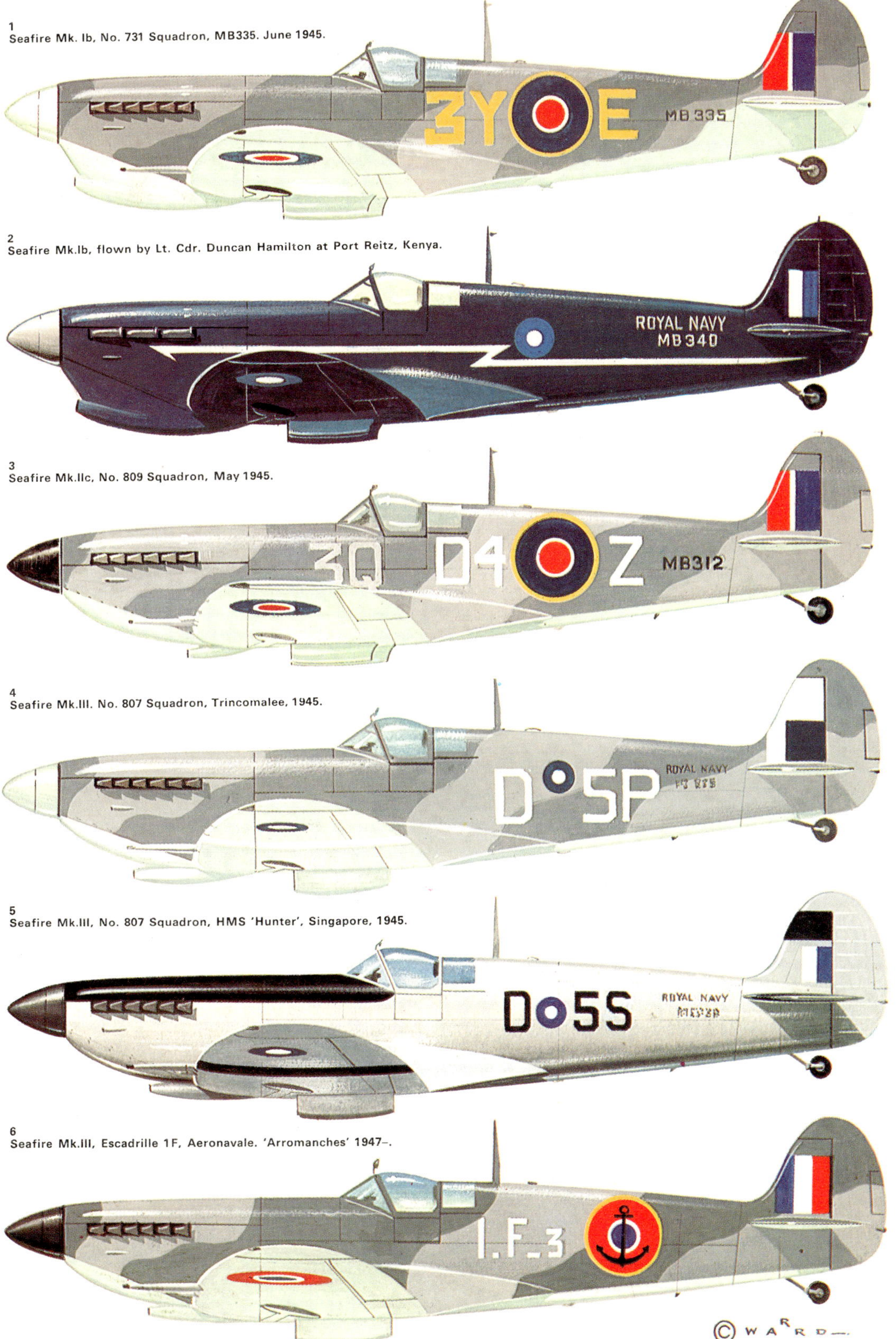

1
Seafire Mk. Ib, No. 731 Squadron, MB335. June 1945.

2
Seafire Mk.Ib, flown by Lt. Cdr. Duncan Hamilton at Port Reitz, Kenya.

3
Seafire Mk.IIc, No. 809 Squadron, May 1945.

4
Seafire Mk.III. No. 807 Squadron, Trincomalee, 1945.

5
Seafire Mk.III, No. 807 Squadron, HMS 'Hunter', Singapore, 1945.

6
Seafire Mk.III, Escadrille 1F, Aeronavale. 'Arromanches' 1947–.

H

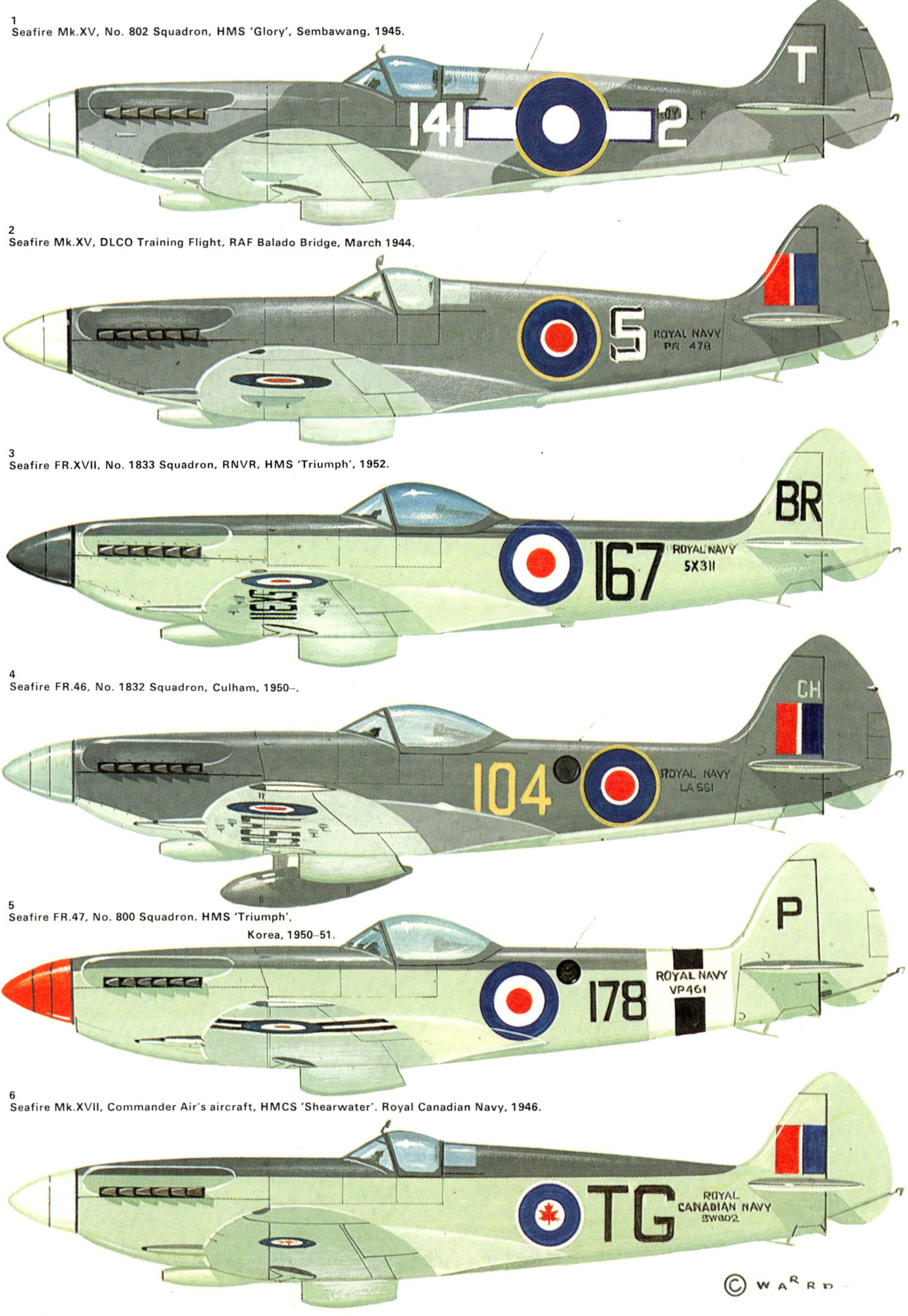

1
Seafire Mk.XV, No. 802 Squadron, HMS 'Glory', Sembawang, 1945.

2
Seafire Mk.XV, DLCO Training Flight, RAF Balado Bridge, March 1944.

3
Seafire FR.XVII, No. 1833 Squadron, RNVR, HMS 'Triumph', 1952.

4
Seafire FR.46, No. 1832 Squadron, Culham, 1950–.

5
Seafire FR.47, No. 800 Squadron, HMS 'Triumph', Korea, 1950–51.

6
Seafire Mk.XVII, Commander Air's aircraft, HMCS 'Shearwater'. Royal Canadian Navy, 1946.

Left: F.XIVE of No. 1 Wing, serial SG3.

Right: Spitfires of an Auxiliary Squadron, note black cannon blisters.

Below: F.XIVE of an unknown unit.

Bottom 3 pictures: Mixed Spitfires of the Coxyde Fighter School. IQ–C SG102; IQ–D SG120; IQ–L SG16. Note F.XIVE SG102 with provision for oblique camera.

Right: Mixed formation from the Coxyde Fighter School. IQ–V SG108; IQ–Y SG112; IQ–M SG117. Note black wing roots on all aircraft.

Below: IQ–N SG104 in white above fin flash, note camouflage pattern and white spinner.

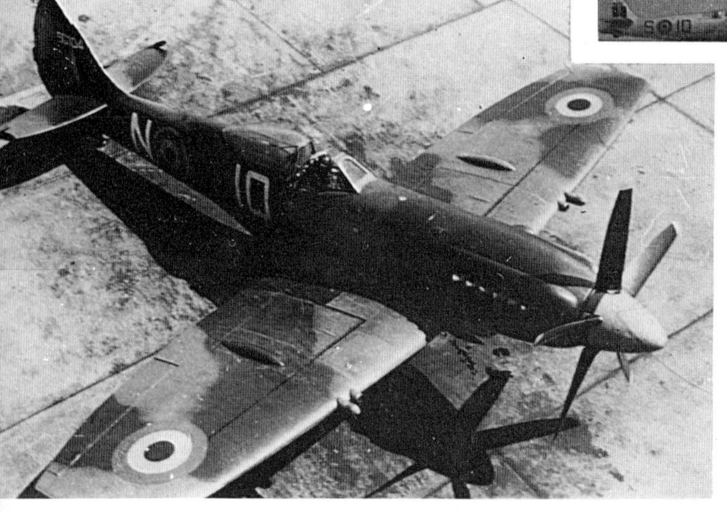

Below: IQ–D somewhat embarrassed, note black cannon blisters, wing roots and anti-glare panel. Serial SG93.

Below: In non-standard camouflage IQ–Z SG127 sporting the insignia of the Fighter School, Coxyde, see colour illustration.

Above: FR.XIVE SG85 in spick and span condition.

Left: CF–GNZ, ex FR.XIVE TZ138, at the Cleveland Air Races in 1949 when it was placed third in the Tinnerman Trophy Race at 359·565 mph. (J. Harvey).

Below: PRXIX of the F.11 Wing, Swedish Air Force. (Bo Widfeldt).

Below: An FR.XIVE supplied to the Royal Thai Air Force in 1948.

Below: F.22 of the Royal Egyptian Air Force.

Seafire IIC of No. 885 Squadron on HMS 'Formidable' with the 'Rock' forming a backdrop. Standard camouflage with sky codes, spinner and under surfaces. (IWM).

SUPERMARINE SEAFIRE Mk.IB-47

It is evident that Supermarine considered the Spitfire as a carrier-based fighter as early as 1940 when the Type 340 design for a " hooked " version was prepared. However, not until late 1941 did this come to fruition when successful deck-landing trials were completed on HMS Illustrious. Orders were then placed in the spring of 1942 for the Seafire IB (conversions of Spitfire VB airframes) and the IIC (production of the Spitfire VC to naval standards).

The Seafire was never to be the world's best carrier fighter, being somewhat too delicate for the continual rigours of deck-landing and rather deficient in range. However, it played a most important role in supplying naval fighter cover until the introduction of the Hellcat and Corsair into operational service with the Royal Navy in 1944. Also, after the War, the Griffon-Seafire provided a nucleus of fighter squadrons with a good aircraft until replacement by the Sea Fury and Attacker.

Production of the Seafire amounted to well over two thousand aircraft (including nearly eight hundred Griffon versions) and, between 1942 and 1953, the Seafire was used by some twenty-eight regular and reserve squadrons on more than twenty carriers of the Royal Navy. Peak operational strength was in the summer of 1943 with eighteen squadrons, many of these operating from eight carriers, mostly in the Mediterranean.

Into Battle 1942 to 1943

Between early July and September 1942, 801, 807, 880, and 885 squadrons began to work-up with the first Seafire Mk's IB and IIC. For the North African landings in November, 801 and 807 embarked in the carrier Furious, and 885 in the Formidable. Of the three squadrons, 807 had the most success in encounters with the Vichy French Air Force.

During the first half of 1943 more squadrons re-equipped with the Mk. IIC, and in July the Seafires of Formidable and Indomitable provided air cover for the landings on Sicily. For the Salerno landing on Italy in September, Formidable was joined by Illustrious (replacing Indomitable), the newly-commissioned Unicorn, and four of the small escort carriers with Seafires. This landing drew a strong reaction from the Germans, and the Seafires played a very crucial role in defending the beachhead during the early days until shore bases could be maintained for the R.A.F. and U.S.A.A.F. Spitfires.

This action saw the introduction of the Seafire III which had folding wings and a strengthened undercarriage. The Mk. III was built in greater numbers than any other variant from 1943 to 1945, replacing the Mk. IIC in 1944. Introduction of the low-altitude rated Merlin 32 and 55M engines on the Westland and Cunliffe-Owen production lines resulted in the LF.III and a few FR.III versions with cameras.

IIC's lined up on HMS 'Formidable', No. 885 Squadron, FAA. (IWM).

Seafire IIC MB293. The odd looking device under the fuselage is a trailing-static 'bomb' for calibrating airspeed during performance testing.

Action in all Theatres 1944 and 1945

In the rough Atlantic waters the use of the Seafires on the small escort carriers had not proved a success and 816, 833, 834, and 842 squadrons re-equipped with Wildcats in the winter of 1943-44. However, operating from the larger carriers: Furious and the new Indefatigable, 801 and 894 gave air cover to the naval air strikes on the Tirpitz in 1944. Also in that year, some U.S. Navy pilots flew Seafires of the Air Spotting Pool, providing direction for the ship bombardment on D-day. In August, four of the seven British escort carriers of Task Force 88, covering the landings in southern France, carried Seafire III's of 807, 809, 879, and 899 squadrons.

Finally in November, with the sinking of the Tirpitz by the R.A.F., the Royal Navy could concentrate on the Far East. Numerous escort carriers arrived in the Indian ocean during 1945 and, four of them carrying Seafires, were engaged on strikes along the Burma coastline. Of the larger fleet carriers, two operated Seafires in the Pacific. HMS Indefatigable with 887 and 894 squadrons was the first to arrive and, after strikes on Sumatra in January, joined the U.S. Navy T.F.57 off Okinawa. In July the Implacable arrived with 801 and 880 squadrons, and both carriers then joined T.F.37 working in Japanese waters. It was in the Pacific that Lt. R. Reynolds of 894 squadron obtained more "kills" to make him the only Seafire pilot to score more than five victories.

As the War ended, the Mk. III was rapidly phased out of service, although a notable exception was the French Naval Air Service, which operated Seafire III's of Flotille 1F from the carrier Arromanches over Indochina in 1948-49. In Ireland, twelve LF.III's of the Air Corps led a very peaceful existence on land from 1947, until retirement in 1955.

The Griffon-Seafires

With the success of the Griffon-Spitfire established by 1943 it was natural that the Royal Navy should be interested in a naval version. Therefore, the Seafire Mk. XV was ordered in that year. This variant was the equivalent of the Spitfire XII, but used the experience gained with the Seafire III, having the folding wings of the latter.

Production commenced in late 1944 but the type never saw wartime service, 802 squadron being reformed with the Mk. XV in England in May 1945, and in the Pacific, 801 received their first aircraft in the following September. No. 803 squadron, transferred to the Royal Canadian Navy, operated Mk. XV's until renumbered 883 squadron in 1947. Flown from Canadian land bases, they were finally transferred to the 1st Training Group at Dartmouth, N.S. The only other country to operate the Mk. XV was Burma which ordered twenty denavalised versions in 1951 to supplement its Spitfires.

Introduction of the Seafire Mk. XVII was rather slow between late 1945 and 1947. This was basically an improved Mk. XV with a strengthened undercarriage, provision for rocket projectiles, and a "tear-drop" canopy. In most cases, the few squadrons equipped with this variant kept their aircraft for only a short period, but the reserve squadrons, 1831 at Stretton and 1832 at Culham, retained some until 1951. No. 764 Training squadron was the very last unit with Seafires, operating the F.17 until November 1954.

The Seafire F.45 and F.46, based on the Spitfire 21 and 22, were only built in small numbers, and, not having folding wings, were relegated to training and reserve flying. The last of the Spitfire/Seafire line was the Seafire FR.47 which remained in production until March 1949. The FR.47 was essentially a very-much modified Spitfire F.24 with folding wings. Only three squadrons were equipped from 1948 onwards: 1833, 804, and 800, in that order. No. 1833 retained their aircraft until the summer of 1953, and 800 flew theirs on ground-attack sorties in Malaya in 1949. In 1950 this squadron re-embarked on HMS Triumph and joined the Korean War, flying the last Seafire combat sorties from late-June to October, 1950.

Seafire IIC MB156, No. 885 Squadron, HMS 'Formidable' well and truly held down whilst the engine is run up prior to take-off. (IWM).

Seafire IB, No. 731 Squadron, see colour illustration.
(K. Atkinson via R. C. Jones).

Seafire L.IIC, No. 808 Squadron, farthest a/c MB312 (M. Garbett).

Seafire L.IIC, No. 809 Squadron, note two codes, 3Q– 808 Sqdn; D4– 809 Squadron. See colour illustration. (via R. C. Jones).

Seafire IIC of No. 885 Squadron, Ø6–B just leaving the catapult on HMS 'Furious'
(D. R. Wheeler via D. J. Brown).

Seafire IIC, No. 885 Squadron with tail well up about to leave the deck of HMS 'Furious'.
(C. H. Wood via R. C. Jones).

Above: Seafire L.III of the Fighter Trainer School Yeovilton. Code Y–9B in yellow. (L. Hunt via M. Garbett).

Left: Seafire L.III, No. 807 Squadron, Trincomalee, Ceylon, 1945. (G. J. Thomas).

Above two pictures & below: Seafire L.III's of No. 807 Squadron, Trincomalee, Ceylon, 1945. Standard finish with sky grey codes except D5–S (centre) which had red. (photos G. E. Thomas via M. Garbett).

Above: Seafire F.XV of No. 803 Squadron, Royal Canadian Navy, landing on HMS 'Warrior', 1946. (Canadian Dept. National Defence).

Right: Good close-up showing bomb rack details of Seafire F.XV of No. 883 Squadron, RCN in Canada in 1947.
(Canadian Dept. National Defence).

Above: Seafire F.XV, PR479, 1st Training Group, Dartmouth, Nova Scotia. The Canadian Seafires were unusual in having an aerial mast for H/T radio rather than the VHF 'whip' type. Note also the radio call-sign letters VG–AAB and its presentation under the wings and on the fuselage. (via F. G. Freeman Jr.).

Below: Seafire F.XV, PR461, 1st Training Group, circa 1948–49. (Canadian Dept. National Defence).

Right: Seafire F.XV, No. 802 Squadron, HMS 'Glory', Sembawang. Note white T on fin indicating HMS 'Glory' and code 141–1. See colour illustration.
(M. Pess via R. C. Jones).

Below: Seafire F.XV, D.L.C.O. Training Flight, RAF Balado Bridge. Serial PR478.
(K. Atkinson via R. C. Jones).

Right: A very smart late-production Seafire F.XV, SW847 built by Westland.

Above: Line-up of Seafire F.XVII's and F.46'2 of No. 1832 Squadron, Culham. (Flight International).

Below: Seafire F.XVII, SX194 from Lee-on-Solent.

Above two pictures: Seafire FR.46, LA561 of No. 1832 Squadron, Culham.
Below: Mixed formation of F.XVII's and F.46's of No. 183 Squadron. See colour illustrations. (photos Flight International).

Seafire FR.47, VP482 of No. 1833 Squadron, Bramcote, 1953.
(via L. Bachelor).

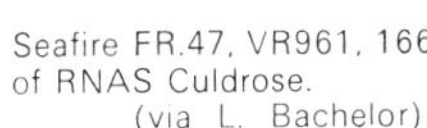

Seafire FR.47, VR961, 166 of RNAS Culdrose.
(via L. Bachelor).

Above: Seafire FR.47's lined-up on the deck of HMS 'Triumph' for a strike against North Korean targets. (IWM).

Below: Seafire FR.47 taking off from the flight deck of HMS 'Triumph' during the Korean War. (IWM).

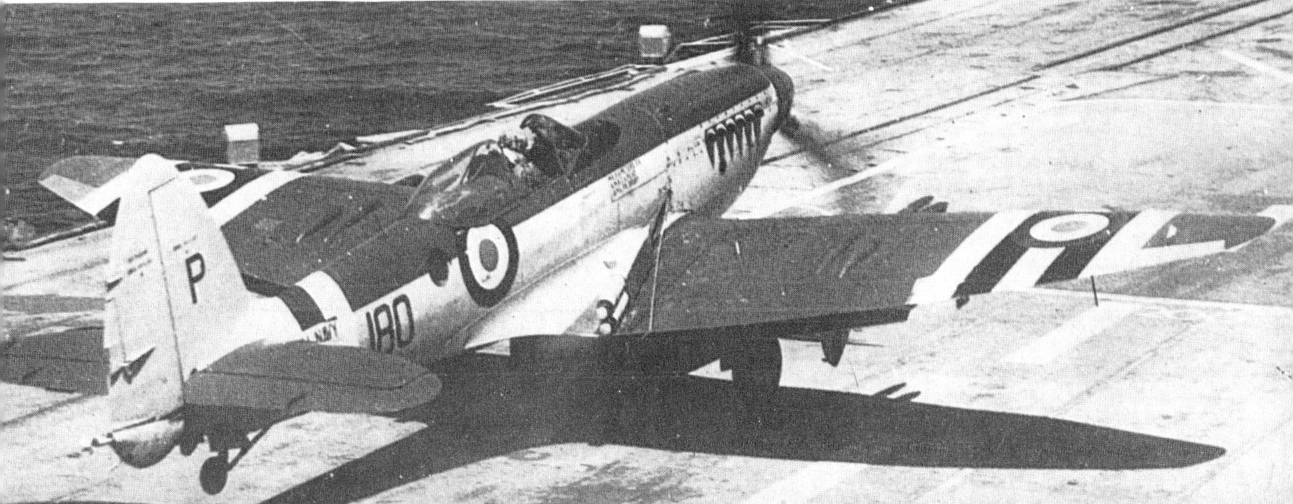

Above: Seafire III of F.22 Aeronavale on the carrier 'Arromanches'. Note size of upper wing roundels. (ECA via R. C. Jones).

Right & below: Seafire III's of F.22 on the flight deck of the 'Arromanches', Aeronavale. (photos ECA via R. C. Jones).

Below: Seafire LF.III's of the Irish Air Corps. (Irish Air Corp).

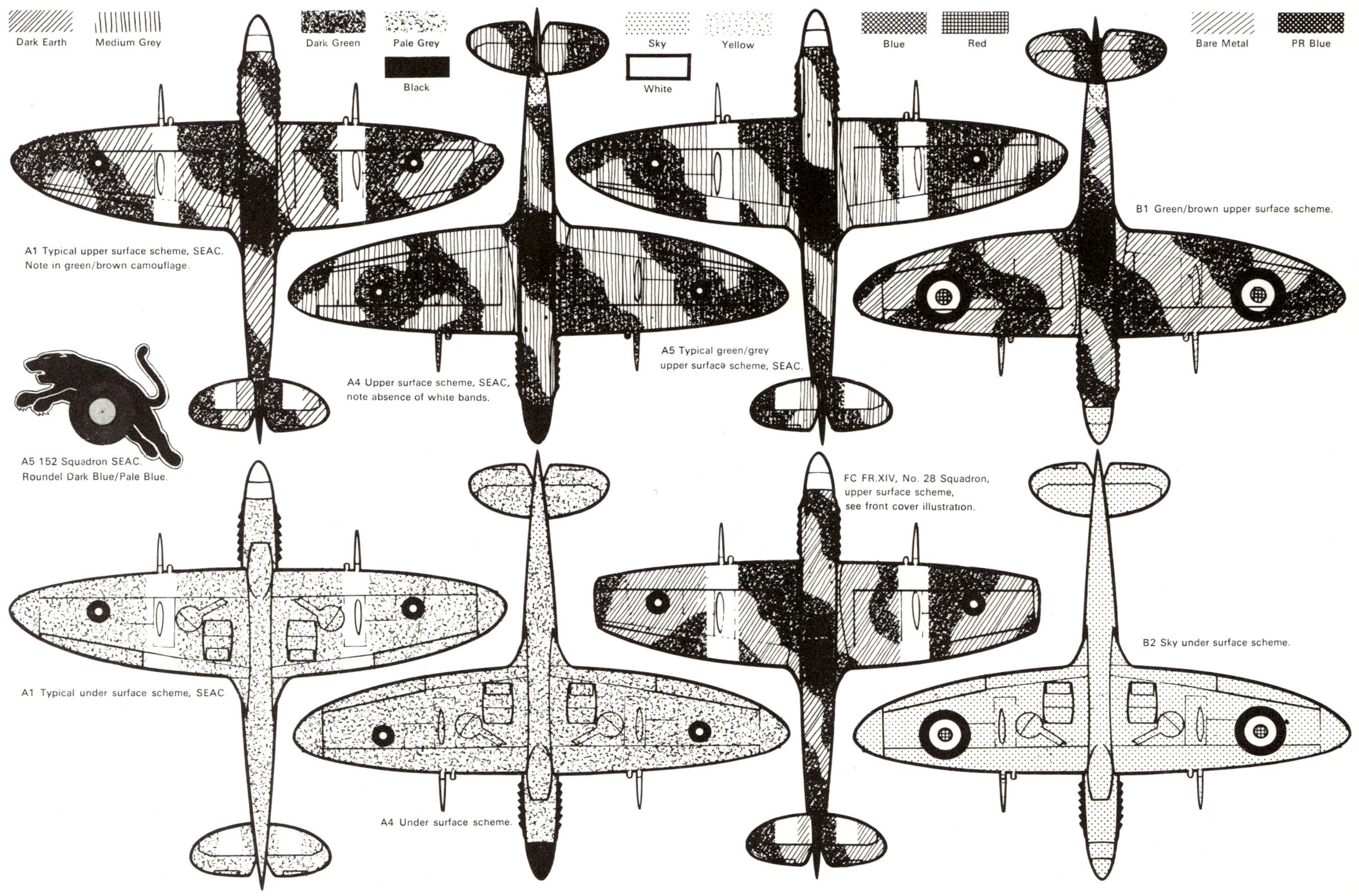

A1 Typical upper surface scheme, SEAC.
Note in green/brown camouflage.

A4 Upper surface scheme, SEAC,
note absence of white bands.

A5 Typical green/grey
upper surface scheme, SEAC.

B1 Green/brown upper surface scheme.

A5 152 Squadron SEAC.
Roundel Dark Blue/Pale Blue.

FC FR.XIV, No. 28 Squadron,
upper surface scheme,
see front cover illustration.

A1 Typical under surface scheme, SEAC.

A4 Under surface scheme.

B2 Sky under surface scheme.

B3 Typical upper surface scheme.

B4 Upper surface scheme.

C1 Under surface scheme, upper surface as B5.

C5 Upper surface detail.

B3 Typical under surface scheme.

B5 Upper surface scheme, note extra ring added to roundel. 2nd TAF.

C4 Upper surface detail, under surface identical but with serial as in C5.

C5 Under surface detail.

C6 Upper surface detail, note large white 4 on port wing.

D2 Upper surface detail, no Invasion stripes under wings.

E1 Standard upper surface scheme, 1945-6.

E2, 6 Upper surface scheme, smaller roundels on E6, under surfaces identical.

D1 Upper surface detail, under surfaces identical but with serial as in C5

D3, 4, 5 Standard post-war PR upper surface scheme.

E1 Under surface scheme.

E4 Standard bare metal scheme, upper surface identical without serials.

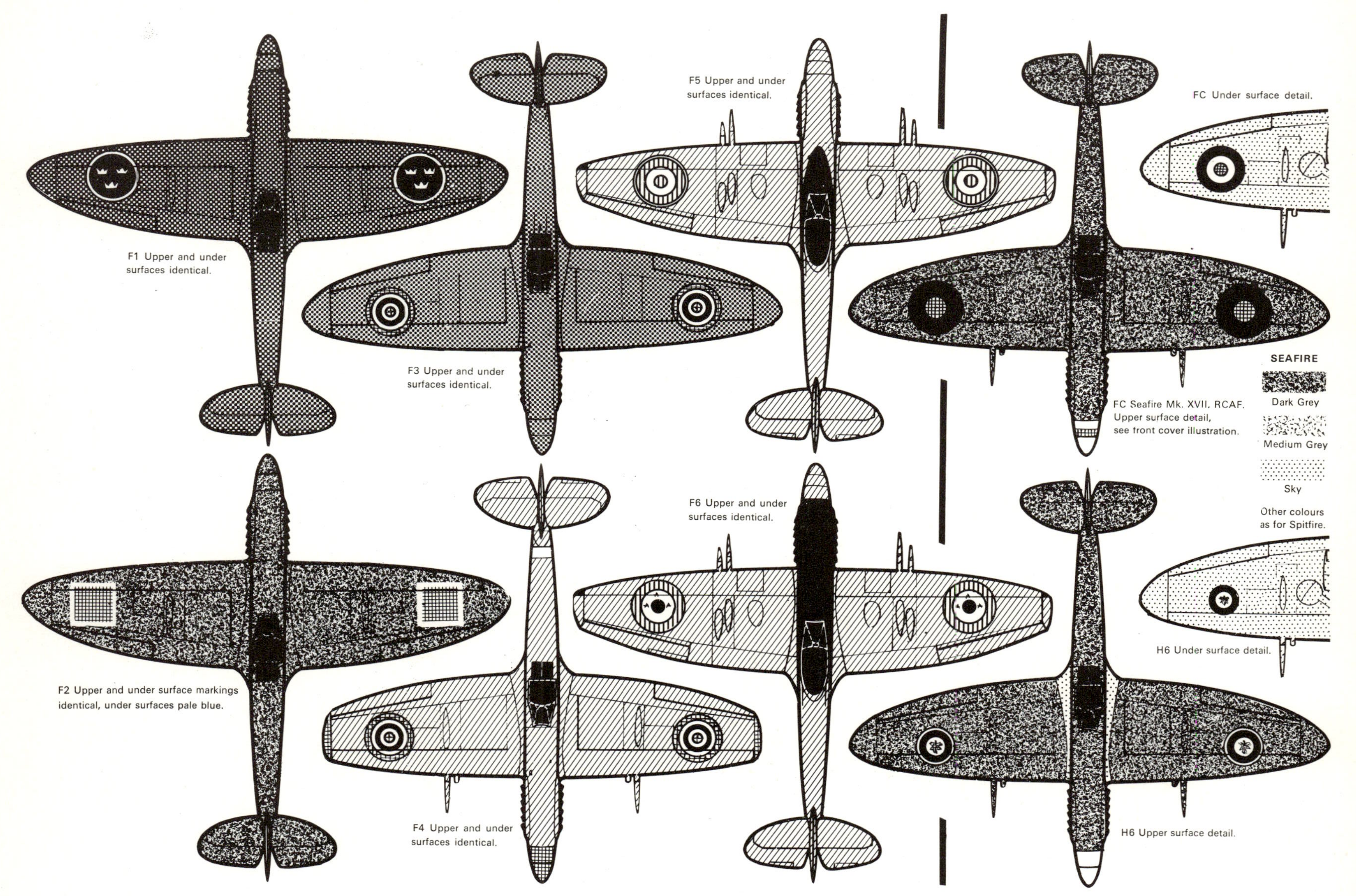
F1 Upper and under surfaces identical.
F3 Upper and under surfaces identical.
F5 Upper and under surfaces identical.
FC Under surface detail.
FC Seafire Mk. XVII. RCAF. Upper surface detail, see front cover illustration.
SEAFIRE
Dark Grey
Medium Grey
Sky
Other colours as for Spitfire.
F2 Upper and under surface markings identical, under surfaces pale blue.
F4 Upper and under surfaces identical.
F6 Upper and under surfaces identical.
H6 Under surface detail.
H6 Upper surface detail.